JANE
GOODALL
LEGENDARY PRIMATOLOGIST

JANE

GOODALL

LEGENDARY PRIMATOLOGIST

by Brenda Haugen

Content Adviser: Randall Susman, Ph.D.,
Department of Anatomical Sciences,
Stony Brook State University of New York

Reading Adviser: Katie Van Sluys, Ph.D.,
Department of Teacher Education,
DePaul University

COMPASS POINT BOOKS MINNEAPOLIS, MINNESOTA

Compass Point Books
3109 West 50th Street, #115
Minneapolis, MN 55410

Visit Compass Point Books on the Internet at *www.compasspointbooks.com*
or e-mail your request to *custserv@compasspointbooks.com*

Editor: Julie Gassman
Photo Researcher: Marcie C. Spence
Designer: Heather Griffin
Library Consultant: Kathleen Baxter

Art Director: Jaime Martens
Creative Director: Keith Griffin
Editorial Director: Carol Jones
Managing Editor: Catherine Neitge

*For Jill Wallin, another brave, curious, and adventurous woman and a
dear, dear friend. I hope you know how much I admire you. BLH*

Library of Congress Cataloging-in-Publication Data
Haugen, Brenda.
  Jane Goodall: legendary primatologist / by Brenda Haugen.
      p. cm.—(Signature lives)
  Includes bibliographical references and index.
  ISBN 0-7565-1590-4 (hard cover)
  1. Goodall, Jane, 1934– —Juvenile literature. 2. Primatologists—
England—Biography—Juvenile literature. I. Title. II. Series.
  QL31.G58.H38 2006
  590.92—dc22   2005030061

Signature Lives

MODERN WORLD

From 1900 to the present day, humanity and the world have undergone major changes. New political ideas resulted in worldwide wars. Fascism and communism divided some countries, and democracy brought others together. Drastic shifts in theories and practice tested the standards of personal freedoms and religious conventions as well as science, technology, and industry. These changes have created a need for world policies and an understanding of international relations. The new mind-set of the modern world includes a focus on humanitarianism and the belief that a global economy has made the world a more connected place.

Table of Contents

1 A WELCOME THIEF

☙❦❧

Someone had stolen the bananas that Jane Goodall was going to have with her evening meal. If she was concerned, it was only for a moment. Her heart leapt when she learned the identity of the culprit—David Greybeard, one of the chimpanzees she'd been studying. According to Goodall's camp cook, the chimpanzee had spent about an hour eating fruit from one of the oil palms that grew nearby. After having his fill of the nutlike fruit, he went into Goodall's tent and took her bananas.

It was the summer of 1961. For a year, Goodall had been studying the chimps living in Gombe Stream Reserve near Lake Tanganyika in Central Africa. She watched the chimps, observed their unique features, and gave them each his or her own

Like humans, a chimpanzee has opposable thumbs, which aid in grabbing a branch or picking up food.

name. But every time she drew closer to them, the chimps ran away in fear. The day a chimp actually visited her camp and was brave enough to enter her tent marked a breakthrough in her work. With hope that David Greybeard would reappear the next day, Goodall put out some bananas and stayed in camp instead of going into the forest as she normally would.

The morning passed without any sign of a chimp. As the afternoon dragged on, Goodall grew disappointed. She feared that David Greybeard's visit might have been a one-time event. However, at around 4 P.M., Goodall heard a noise in the bushes across from her tent. She watched as David Greybeard entered the camp. Just like the day before, he went to one of the oil palms and began eating nuts. When he'd had his fill, the chimp took the bananas that Goodall had left for him.

During the next five days, the calm and curious chimp came to Goodall's camp to eat nuts three times. Each time he visited, he'd also help himself to bananas that

Found in the tropical areas of western Africa, Central America, and South America, the oil palm can grow to 66 feet (20 meters) tall. The leaves of the tree stretch from nearly 10 feet (3 m) to 16 ½ feet (5 m). Oil palms produce a nutlike fruit with a fleshy outer layer and a single seed inside. This fruit is rich in nutrients, making it an important food for many animals, including a bird called the palm nut vulture. The fruit is also used to make vegetable oil for cooking or food processing.

she put out for him. About a month later, David Greybeard began feasting on the nuts that he spotted in another tree at camp. During one of these visits, the big chimp with the dense white beard showed even more trust toward his camp host. He took a banana right from Goodall's hand.

Jane Goodall continued to observe David Greybeard until his death in 1968.

David Greybeard's trust in Goodall made her research a great deal easier. The chimp no longer feared her and even approached her out in the forest. After seeing him interacting with Goodall, the other

The study of animals is called zoology. Within the field of zoology there are multiple, varied branches of study. For example, zoological studies include paleontology (the study of prehistoric organisms), physiology (the study of the physical functions of animals), and ecology (the study of animals' relationships to their environments). Jane Goodall's research fell into the study of instinctive animal behavior, a field known as ethology. Her work also falls into the field of primatology, the study of the behavior, development, and origin of primates.

chimps became less afraid. In time, they let her get closer to them, too.

As Goodall continued her studies of the chimps, she made discoveries about the animals that surprised the scientific community. She found that chimps are more like human beings than scientists had once believed. Today, more than 45 years after she first set foot in Gombe, Goodall's research continues, and she's known worldwide as the foremost expert on the behavior of chimpanzees.

Goodall's career began as a childhood wish to see African animals in their natural environments. As an adult, she made that wish come true through hard work and perseverance. She also opened the door for other women to become ethologists, scientists who study animal behavior.

Even in 2005, at the age of 71, Goodall continued to work tirelessly, traveling around the globe to share her wealth of experience. She is a spokesperson for conserving great apes and other animals in their natural environments, as well as

Jane Goodall communicates with a chimp in a German zoo in 2004.

in captivity. She hopes that by understanding more about the creatures of the world, people will learn the importance of respecting and protecting animals and their environments. In the process, she hopes the world will become a better place for every living thing. 🦋

2 A CURIOUS CHILD

Chapter

❧❧❧

For as long as she could remember, Valerie Jane Goodall dreamed of getting a close-up view of all the wondrous, wild animals of Africa. Though her home in England seemed a world away from the African habitats and species in her dream, Valerie Jane's mother, Vanne, always encouraged her to work to make her wishes come true.

Valerie Jane Goodall—"V.J." to her childhood friends, and "Jane" as she grew older—was born in London, England, on April 3, 1934. When Jane was 2 years old, the Goodalls, along with Jane's nanny, moved to a house just outside of the city.

In the early 1930s, Jane's father, Mortimer, worked as a telephone cable-testing engineer in London. He didn't find his job very satisfying, and he longed for some excitement in his work. He found it as a race-car driver. In 1939, the Goodall family—which now included Jane's 1-year-old sister, Judy—moved to France to live closer to the European tracks where Mortimer raced. After just a few months, however, the situation grew tense as Adolf Hitler and his Nazis posed a serious threat to Europeans. The Goodalls decided they'd be safer moving back to England. Because their former home had been sold, the family moved to

Mortimer raced in the 24-hour Le Mans endurance race several times.

the large, old country manor where Mortimer had been raised.

They hadn't been living in their country home long when Jane disappeared one day. Her family searched for her for hours and was ready to call the police when they spotted the 5-year-old girl. Vanne later wrote:

> *I don't remember who saw her first—a small, dishevelled figure coming a little wearily over the ... field by the hen houses. There were bits of straw in her hair and on her clothes but her eyes, dark ringed with fatigue, were shining.*

As the relieved family gathered around Jane, her mother asked where she'd been. Jane excitedly explained she'd spent the last five hours watching and waiting to see a hen lay an egg. She wanted to know where the eggs that she helped gather came from, and rather than just ask, she decided to solve the mystery for herself.

A big pen enclosed five henhouses on the manor's property. Jane had patiently waited inside one of the small buildings as a hen came inside and sat on a nest of straw about 5 feet (1.5 m) in front of her. Despite the heat and smell, Jane sat silently, not daring to move and disturb the hen. Her patience paid off as she watched the hen raise herself from the nest. A white egg slowly fell from the feathers between the hen's legs and landed on the straw.

Though stiff from sitting still so long, Jane's excitement enabled her to run back to the house to tell her story to her mother. Instead of being angry that Jane had neglected to tell anyone where she was going, Vanne listened with excitement, too, as Jane told her tale. It would prove to be the first of many animal behavior observations for Jane.

These easygoing days in the country soon came to an end. On September 1, 1939, Germany invaded Poland. Just days later, England and France came to Poland's aid by declaring war on Germany. World War II had begun, and Mortimer joined the British army.

Not long after that, the family's nanny got married and started a new life. Vanne, Jane, and Judy moved to The Birches, a manor owned by Vanne's family in Bournemouth in southern England. After the war ended, Mortimer continued to work as a race-car driver, traveling around Europe's racing circuit. Eventually, the distance between Mortimer and

World War II devastated much of Europe and Asia before it ended in 1945. About 17 million soldiers died in the conflict between the Allies—which included the United States, England, France, and the Soviet Union—and the Axis powers—Germany, Italy, and Japan. Civilians died in even greater numbers because of bombing attacks, starvation, and disease.

Vanne led to divorce.

Jane spent most of her time with her mother. She loved growing up at The Birches, but she didn't like school nearly as much. Although she did well in her classes, she preferred to be outdoors, watching birds or climbing trees.

In the winter months, when much of the outdoors was sleeping, Jane loved to read. Her favorite books were *The Story of Doctor Dolittle*, *The Jungle Book*, and tales about Tarzan. In her autobiography,

A print from a 1903 edition of The Jungle Book, *one of Jane's favorite tales*

Jane later wrote:

We couldn't afford many new books, but we belonged to the local library. One day for my weekend library book Mum brought me The Story of Doctor Dolittle, *by Hugh Lofting. I read it all the way through. Then I read it through again. I had never before loved a book so much. I read it a third time before it had to go back—I finished it under the bedclothes*

Author Hugh Lofting created a number of illustrations for his book, The Story of Doctor Dolittle.

with a flashlight after Mum had turned off the light. That was in November. And I shall never forget that (Grandma) Danny gave me the book for my very own that Christmas. I was seven years old. I think that was when I first decided I must go to Africa someday.

At age 12, Jane decided to start her own nature group, named the Alligator Club. The club consisted of four members—Jane, her sister, Judy, and their friends Sally and Sue Cary, who often visited during summers and holidays. The girls camped in the backyard garden, went on nature walks, and took note of the birds and insects they saw. Jane even created a club magazine, the *Alligator Society Magazine*, filled with drawings of insects and notes on other things members had noticed in nature. Jane also sent out nature quizzes the girls could fill out for fun.

One summer, the girls of the Alligator Club created their own museum. Included in the exhibits were pressed flowers and shells, but the big draw was a human skeleton, borrowed from Jane's uncle,

During World War I, Hugh Lofting served in the British army. In letters to his children, he wrote about Doctor Dolittle, a character he created for their amusement. In 1920, the first of Lofting's Doctor Dolittle books was published. It told the tale of a doctor who could talk to animals. The book became so popular, a dozen more would follow. In 1967, a musical film based on the books was released. It was nominated for an Academy Award for best picture and won Academy Awards for best effects, special effects, and best song.

who was a surgeon. They opened their museum to anyone who wanted to visit, but they asked for contributions as admission. The money was donated to an organization that sent old horses to farms where they could comfortably live out their lives. This rescued the old animals from being butchered.

Jane also regularly walked a collie named Budleigh for a woman who ran a candy store. On one of their walks, they met Rusty, a dog that lived in a local hotel. Rusty started joining Jane and Budleigh on their trips to the beach. Along with giving Budleigh some exercise, Jane tried to teach him some tricks. Thinking Rusty wasn't very smart, Jane didn't try to teach him anything—but he watched as Jane worked with Budleigh. To Jane's surprise, Rusty learned not only all the tricks she taught Budleigh, but also some other remarkable feats, including climbing up tall ladders and closing doors.

Jane had a way with animals, and she and Rusty developed a close relationship. Though he still lived at the hotel, Rusty came to Jane's front door in the morning and barked to let her know he had arrived. With the permission of Rusty's owners, they'd spend the day together.

The time she spent with Rusty led Jane to realize that dogs can think and solve problems. She also

African scenery filled Jane's dreams of her future.

believed Rusty had feelings similar to some human emotions. Unlike many animals, Rusty loved to be dressed up. But if someone laughed at him when he was dressed up, he'd walk away, shedding the clothes as he went. He also acted like he was sorry whenever he did something wrong but sulked when he was accused of something he didn't do.

Jane's interest in animals continued throughout her childhood. When she completed high school, it was time to decide what she would do with her life. What would her calling be, and how could she fulfill her dream of traveling to Africa? ✑

3 AFRICA BOUND

Chapter

❧⋯❧

Vanne Goodall gave her daughter a valuable piece of advice. She told Jane that if she became a secretary, she could get a job anywhere in the world. So Jane went to secretarial school in London and earned her diploma.

In the spring of 1954, Goodall began her first secretarial job at her aunt's clinic for children with polio, muscular dystrophy, and other illnesses. Doctors traveled to the clinic each week to work with their patients. Goodall's job was to type letters for the visiting doctors. She wrote:

> *I learned so much at that clinic. Ever since then, when things have gone wrong in my life, I remember how lucky I am to be healthy. And I feel a special closeness*

Louis Leakey was a great mentor in Jane Goodall's life.

Oxford University is in Oxford, a town about 50 miles (80 km) from London.

with people who are crippled or disabled in any way.

Six months later, Goodall was excited to get a job working in the filing department of Oxford University. She had wanted to take classes there, but she couldn't afford the tuition. She considered working at the university to be "the next best thing." She lived with some Oxford students and met many more. She had the social life of a college student without taking the classes.

After a year, Goodall returned to London, where she had accepted an interesting and challenging job at a film studio called Schofield Productions. Here she learned some new skills and enjoyed her work, choosing music for documentaries and helping with editing and other tasks. During her free time, she visited the Natural History Museum and read books about animals, particularly those from Africa.

Her dream of seeing Africa's wild animals inched closer to reality in May 1956 when Goodall received a letter from school friend Marie Claude "Clo" Mange. In her letter, Mange invited her for a visit to Kenya, a country on the east coast of Africa. Mange's parents had bought a farm there and welcomed a visit from Mange's old school chum.

Goodall jumped at the chance, but first she needed to earn money

It was not uncommon for Europeans to own land in Kenya during the 1950s. In the late 1890s, the British government took control of Kenya, and the area was known as British East Africa. A railroad was built across the country, and Europeans were encouraged to settle and establish farms in Kenya. During the 1940s, Africans began opposing the British rule, and in 1963, Kenya achieved independence after years of rebel activity led by the Mau Mau movement.

for her journey. Though she loved her job at the film studio, she didn't earn much there. Goodall decided to quit her job and move back home with her mother where she could live for free. Then she took a job as a waitress at a hotel called the Hawthorns and saved every bit she could. About four months after moving home, she counted the money she'd hidden under the carpet in the drawing room. She finally had enough to pay for her trip to Africa.

Twenty-three-year-old Goodall boarded a steamship called the *Kenya Castle* that was headed for Mombasa, Kenya. She later wrote:

> *I wanted the trip to go on forever. I loved being up on deck, where I watched the sea and glimpsed dolphins, sharks, and flying fish. I especially loved it when it was rough and most passengers were in their cabins. I was lucky. I never felt seasick.*

The trip to Kenya took three weeks, but Goodall's journey didn't end at the port in Mombasa. She had to travel by train to the capital city of Nairobi. She loved every minute of the two-day journey. Looking out the window, Goodall got a taste of the countryside and even saw some of the area's wild animals in the distance.

Mange met Goodall in Nairobi and took her to her family's farm. Along the way, Goodall spotted her

Kenyan women shopping in Nairobi in the 1950s

first wild giraffe. Amazed and excited, Goodall knew her childhood dream was coming true.

She spent three weeks with Mange's family, but she had no intention of returning home right away. Before she had even left England, she had secured a job at the Kenyan office of a large international company. While Goodall was not impressed with the job, she didn't care. She was able to earn enough to live in Kenya and continue searching for a job in which she could work with animals. She wrote home in April 1957:

> I really do simply adore Kenya. It is so wild, uncultivated, primitive, mad, exciting, unpredictable. It is also slightly degrading in its effect on some rather weak characters, but on the whole I am living in the Africa I have always longed for, always felt stirring in my blood.

Louis Leakey (1903–1972) was born near Nairobi, Kenya. His parents were British missionaries. Like Goodall, his career started with a childhood dream when he discovered his first fossils as a 12-year-old. He studied anthropology, the study of human culture, at Cambridge University. His work focused on learning about the earliest human beings to roam the earth.

With a little luck and perseverance, Goodall soon met a man who could help her realize her goals. Mange knew of Goodall's interest in animals and had told her about Louis Leakey, a well-known anthropologist and paleontologist. Leakey worked as curator of the natural history museum in Nairobi. Goodall called Leakey and arranged to meet with him. As luck would have it, Leakey needed to replace a secretary who was quitting, and after he met with Goodall, he offered her the job.

Through her work with Leakey, Goodall learned more about Kenya's wildlife. She accompanied

him on excursions around Nairobi National Park. He also invited her to join him and his wife, Mary, on their annual expedition to dig for fossils at the Olduvai Gorge in Tanganyika. Along with his interest in animals, Leakey wanted to learn more about early man. He believed humans originated in Africa and hoped to find fossils to back up his thoughts. He enlisted Goodall's help in excavating fossils in

One of Louis and Mary Leakey's great achievements was the discovery of a skull that was estimated to be 600,000 years old.

Serengeti National Park. Goodall found the digging to be difficult work, but she enjoyed this new adventure and spending time with the Leakeys. She wrote to her family in July 1957:

> *I never, never dreamt that I would ever be out in the wilds excavating animal bones from thousands of years before. It is sometimes very hard work—we spent two solid days with pick-axes getting one of the sites ready before we could start digging. Then one uses a sheath knife until one finds a bone, after which you use a dental pick—really.*

Leakey believed that in addition to studying fossils, studying apes could help him answer his questions about how early humans lived. After getting to know Goodall better, he became convinced she could succeed in studying a group of chimps living in Gombe Stream Reserve, a protected area of forest on the eastern side of Lake Tanganyika. He recognized her curiosity about the animal world, her determination to find answers to questions, and her incredible patience as the right combination for the work that needed to be done.

Goodall jumped at the opportunity, but money was needed for travel costs, food and other supplies, and guides to help her find her way through this new environment. Leakey found it difficult to secure

funding for the project, mainly because Goodall had no formal scientific training or experience studying wild animals. She was a secretary. But he didn't give up. He knew she was the right person for the job.

Unlike many other scientists at the time, Leakey believed Goodall's lack of formal training would prove to be a benefit. She could go to the area with no preconceived ideas about what she'd discover. He believed the fact that she was a woman also would be

Leakey, who had grown up in Kenya, was familiar with the region and its vast resources of animal life.

Leakey wanted Goodall to study chimps in what today is Gombe National Park.

a plus. In chimpanzee culture, males are dominant. A female researcher would likely be less threatening to the chimps than a male researcher would be, Leakey thought. After all, in Africa, the hunters were men, and Leakey realized that animals, especially intelligent primates, could tell the difference between men and women.

While Leakey worked to find financing, Goodall traveled back to England, intent on learning more about chimpanzees. She read everything she could get her hands on regarding the animals' behavior, but no one had studied chimps in the wild as intensely as she planned to do. Most of the information she found documented the lives of chimps kept in labs or as pets. Goodall took a job at the London Zoo working in the film library. In her spare time, she studied the zoo's chimps. She didn't like seeing the chimps in their zoo environment and vowed she'd someday help chimps in zoos live in better conditions.

While Goodall worked in England, Leakey secured a $3,000 grant from the Wilkie Foundation that would allow the chimp study to begin. Based in Des Plaines, Illinois, the foundation provided grants for people to study human and nonhuman primates.

Leakey also had to seek permission from British officials to allow the study in the Gombe Stream Reserve. Since the end of World War I, the British had governed the area, and Goodall needed permission from Geoffrey Browning, the British district commissioner, to begin her work. After much persuasion from Leakey, Browning finally gave his OK, on the condition Goodall not go alone. Studying wild chimps could prove dangerous. Though not as tall as adult humans, chimps are much stronger. And several other potentially dangerous creatures called the area home, too, including African buffalo,

> *A chimpanzee's height can range from just over 3 feet (90 centimeters) to 5 feet (165 cm). The animals can weigh anywhere from about 90 pounds (40.5 kilograms) for an adult female to 110 pounds (49.5 kg) for an adult male.*

leopards, and several different kinds of poisonous snakes. Goodall's mother, Vanne, had also visited and fallen in love with Africa, so she volunteered to accompany Jane to Gombe.

About a year after leaving Kenya, Goodall returned to Africa with her mother. On May 31, 1960, the two boarded a plane for Nairobi—only to be met by bad news. Leakey informed them about current disputes regarding fishing rights in Gombe that were making the situation there dangerous. As they waited for the tensions to calm, Jane and Vanne headed west to Lake Victoria. Leakey believed that studying the vervet monkeys at the lake's Lolui Island and

Vervet monkeys develop strong lifelong bonds with female relatives.

recording observations in a notebook would provide Goodall with some important practice in field study:

> *The short study taught me a good deal about such things as note-taking in the field, the sort of clothes to wear, the movements a wild monkey will tolerate in a human observer and those it will not.*

The young woman quickly grew to love Lolui Island and the monkeys that inhabited it. In less than two weeks, she was able to get close to the group of monkeys she chose to observe. But her stay there would be short-lived. On June 30, Leakey radioed that the trip to Gombe was back on track. Goodall and her mother headed back to Nairobi, where she shared her notes with Leakey and packed for the 800-mile (1,200-km) trip to the Tanganyika Territory and the chimpanzees of Gombe. ❧

At the end of World War I, Great Britain controlled and named the territory of Tanganyika. The territory fell under United Nations' trust in 1946, and Great Britain was given the responsibility of preparing Tanganyika to be independent. In 1961, independence was won. Three years later, Tanganyika joined with a group of islands called Zanzibar and became the United Republic of Tanzania.

4 GOMBE AT LAST

Chapter

❧❦❧

On July 16, 1960, Jane, Vanne, and their African cook, Dominic Charles Bandola, arrived at the Gombe Stream Reserve. Two African game scouts helped them find a good campsite in a shady spot near a stream. By the time Goodall had her tent up and supplies put away, it was late afternoon. She decided to explore the area around camp. She later wrote:

> *I shall never forget the thrill of that first exploration. Soon after leaving camp I met a troop of baboons. They were afraid of the strange, white-skinned creature (that was I) and gave their barking alarm call, 'Waa-hoo! Waa-hoo!' again and again. I left them, hoping that they would become used to me soon—otherwise, I thought, all the creatures of Gombe would be frightened.*

Most of Goodall's early days at Gombe were spent on what she calls "the Peak."

The Gombe Stream Reserve is composed of about 20 square miles (52 square kilometers) of land on the eastern side of Lake Tanganyika. It includes more than a dozen streams and rugged, steep terrain. In 1960, more forests surrounded the area but have since been cut down. Some of the animals found in the area when Jane Goodall first arrived— including African buffalo, crocodiles, and hippos—no longer live there, mainly because of human encroachment and destruction of their habitats. In 1968, the reserve was designated a national park.

The next day, Goodall armed herself with a notebook and binoculars and journeyed into the wilderness to find chimpanzees. Because she was told by a British game ranger not to travel in the mountains alone, one of the game scouts joined her.

At first, just spotting one of the chimpanzees provided a thrill. She saw two that day, but she couldn't get close. This would be the case for months. Every time Goodall drew near, the chimps would run away. But she kept trying to earn their trust by being around and being patient. She also begged the game ranger to allow her to travel alone throughout Gombe. After she promised that she'd always let others know where she was going before she left camp, the ranger grudgingly said she could travel through the forests alone.

Goodall found a peak that provided her with a beautiful 360-degree view of the area. She used her binoculars to watch the chimps living their daily lives. In time, she discovered that the chimps

moved around in small groups, usually composed of six or fewer animals. Sometimes, particularly when they found a good food source, chimps banded together into larger groups. Goodall came to realize that the chimps she was watching every day from the peak were part of a community of about 50. She also learned what the chimps ate. She watched as they fed on nuts, fruit, seeds, leaves, and other greens.

While Goodall continued to keep her distance from the chimps, she sometimes ran into other wildlife. One morning as the sun was beginning to rise, she went to the peak as she had so many

A common behavior in daily chimp life is grooming, in which the animals help rid each other of external parasites, as well as reinforce bonds among one another.

> *The African buffalo are huge animals, weighing about 1,500 pounds (675 kg). Their size—along with their large, rigid horns with which they stab their victims—makes them dangerous animals. They are unpredictable and have been known to attack people. Even an armed hunter is in danger of dying from a buffalo attack.*

other days. As she neared the spot where she normally set up her observations, she noticed a large, dark shape about 10 yards (9 m) in front of her. As she focused in on the creature, she realized it was a buffalo. Goodall always moved as quietly as possible through the forest, so the animal didn't hear her or catch her scent. He just calmly continued chewing his cud. Goodall quietly and slowly retreated, never alerting the buffalo to her presence.

On another occasion, Goodall heard a mewing noise as she gazed out from the peak. About 15 yards (13.6 m) from her, the tip of a leopard's tail showed above the tall grass. Quietly, Goodall slipped away and decided to look for chimps in another part of the reserve that day. But nothing could keep her from returning to the peak. Sometimes she even slept there, not letting her fears get the best of her.

As Jane studied Gombe's chimpanzees, Vanne kept busy by setting up a clinic in camp. Area residents who were sick quickly found their way to her. Vanne's clinic proved valuable to the local people and to Jane. People realized Goodall and her

staff were in Gombe to help. Vanne, who would go back to England in November, knew that her work would lead the local residents to want to repay her by helping her daughter when she needed it. 🐾

The buffalo is one of Africa's "Big Five" animals, along with the elephant, rhino, lion, and leopard.

5 | AMAZING DISCOVERIES

Chapter

～◦✕◦～

As she expected, Jane Goodall found more success studying the chimpanzees on her own than with a guide.

As she observed these creatures, Goodall began noticing differences among them. Each looked different from the other, and each boasted a unique personality. As Goodall began to be able to tell the chimps apart, she gave them names, defying a scientific principle of assigning them numbers.

In October 1960, Goodall received a visit from George and Kay Schaller. The Schallers had just finished a groundbreaking study of mountain gorillas in Rwanda and were interested in Goodall's work. Goodall wrote to her family:

George said he thought that if I could see chimps eating meat, or using a tool, a whole year's work would be justified. Well, yesterday we were lucky enough to see a male chimp with a piece of pink meat. I think it was a baby animal of some sort. In the tree with him were a female with a tiny baby clinging round her, and a 6 year old child—and a small collection of baboons. It was the funniest thing. At first it was all rather noisy—the baboons & chimps were chasing each other. But it quieted down, leaving Pa with his meat, and all the others sitting round gazing at him. His wife beseechingly put out her hand, but he tucked the meat firmly under his arm. She made no other move—just sat, gazing longingly, & occasionally putting out her hand & touching his. No response. But he did let the child have a taste. The comical thing was that he sat with the meat in one hand & a bunch of leaves in the other, taking a bite at each, alternating.

Before Goodall's observations, scientists didn't know chimpanzees were meat eaters. In fact, anthropologists thought that one of the things that distinguished humans from apes was the human

tendency to hunt and eat meat.

But this wasn't her only important discovery. She also saw chimps not only using tools but making them. Goodall watched in amazement as the chimps stripped the leaves off of long twigs and then used the twigs to fish termites out of their mounds and eat them. They also created sponges out of chewed leaves to soak up moisture in the hollows of tree trunks when the water level

Goblin, once the high-ranking male in Gombe, eats baboon meat.

A young chimp
uses a leaf to
collect water
and drink.

became too low to be sucked up with their lips. And when fruits proved too difficult to crack open by biting, chimps used rocks or sticks to break them open.

Like meat eating, tool behavior was considered

to be a defining trait of humans before Goodall's observations. These early findings changed the very definition of ape versus human.

From the start, Goodall's work had a great impact on the fields of ethology, ecology, animal behavior, conservation, and anthropology. Her amazing discoveries led to more grants that would allow her to continue her work. On March 13, 1961, she received a $1,400 grant from the National Geographic Society's Committee for Research & Exploration. It became the first in a string of more than two dozen grants she would receive from the National Geographic Society.

Based in Washington, D.C., the National Geographic Society formed in 1888 to gather and share geographic information worldwide. It is the world's largest non-profit scientific and educational association and continues to support research projects around the globe.

In the summer of 1961, the chimp she had named David Greybeard visited Goodall's camp for the first time, which proved to be another turning point in her study. As he grew to trust her, Goodall found she could get closer to the other chimps she was studying as well. She did everything she could think of to build trust and help the chimpanzees be comfortable with her presence. She wore drab-colored clothes that wouldn't cause alarm, and she moved in slow, nonthreatening ways. In time, David

Greybeard brought other chimps to camp, including Goliath and Flo. These chimps also allowed Goodall to get closer to them in the forest.

After spending a year studying Gombe's chimpanzees, Goodall had learned more about these creatures than anyone else ever had. Leakey realized the value of her work, but he also knew some would never take it seriously because she hadn't earned a college degree. Armed with his own reputation as a renowned scientist and a list of Goodall's accomplishments in Gombe, Leakey lobbied officials at Cambridge University in England to allow her to attend. In 1962, Goodall was admitted as a Ph.D. student at the university, a rare honor for someone who had never been to college. When she completed the program in 1966, she would be Dr. Jane Goodall, a college graduate with a degree in ethology, the science of animal behavior.

Meanwhile, Goodall didn't want to miss any valuable information in Gombe while she studied in England. To avoid this problem, she set up a program in which visiting students would continue to track and note the chimps' behavior in

Cambridge University began in 1209 after several scholars left Oxford University following a dispute with local townspeople. A long-standing rivalry between the two universities continues today. Currently, about 12,500 students attend one of Cambridge's 31 colleges. Entrance requirements are highly selective, and the academics are among the most challenging in the world.

Cambridge University on a summer day in the early 1960s

her absence. With the success of this program, the Gombe Stream Research Centre was born. Since the Centre's initiation in 1964, hundreds of students interested in Goodall's work have been able to participate themselves.

Back in England in early 1962, however, Goodall was deeply enthralled in academic activity. Her schedule during her first term at Cambridge was packed. Writing reports, completing other class work, and meeting regularly with her adviser filled her days. She also wrote articles about her work at Gombe for publication and was invited to speak at scientific conferences in England and the United States.

Goodall finished her first term at Cambridge in June 1962 and returned to Gombe for the rest of the year. Even back in Africa, Goodall's life was not the same as it had been before her amazing discoveries. *National Geographic* magazine wanted to document her work and asked to send a photographer. Goodall recalled:

Hugo van Lawick knew he wanted to work with animals in some way from the time he was a young boy. When he settled on filmmaking, he started as a cameraman for film companies in Kenya. He went on to film wildlife in East Africa for the National Geographic Society before working with Jane Goodall.

The National Geographic Society … wanted to send out a professional photographer, but I was terrified at the thought of a stranger arriving on the scene and ruining my hard-won relationship with the chimps.

Despite her concerns, she relented. In August 1962, Dutch photographer Baron Hugo van Lawick came to Gombe. Goodall's worries quickly faded as van Lawick fit in perfectly. Goodall began writing an article about her

A 1996 photo of Hugo van Lawick

work to go along with van Lawick's photographs. In August 1963, "My Life Among Wild Chimpanzees" appeared in *National Geographic*. It proved to be the first of many articles that brought Goodall and her work with the chimpanzees of Gombe to the attention of the general public.

6 A New Partnership

Chapter

During the time they spent together while working on the *National Geographic* article, Jane Goodall and Hugo van Lawick fell in love. They married on March 28, 1964. On top of their wedding cake was a clay model of David Greybeard. Big color portraits of other Gombe chimps, including favorites Goliath, Flo, and Fifi, graced the reception hall.

Goodall and van Lawick shared a love of animals and of the environment. They worked together on the project at Gombe as well as a variety of projects that took them to other parts of Africa.

Goodall continued to gain attention for her work at Gombe. More articles followed the first *National Geographic* submission, and in December 1965, CBS aired a television special called *Miss Goodall and*

A chimp named Fifi searches Goodall, looking for a banana in a photograph by Hugo van Lawick.

Both van Lawick and Goodall were completely at ease in the African wild.

the Wild Chimpanzees. Though public speaking wasn't her favorite thing to do, she followed all the publicity with a lecture tour in the United States and England. The time away made her appreciate her life in Gombe even more.

Goodall added more staff as the research center in Gombe grew. In 1965, the National Geographic Society paid for the construction of new buildings at the Gombe camp, including a special banana storehouse. Goodall had used bananas as tools to gain the chimpanzees' trust and get closer to them. However, the plan had begun to backfire. Chimps and baboons had begun invading the Gombe camp and tore the contents of tents apart in search of bananas. Van Lawick helped Goodall design various banana feeders that released the fruit only when researchers wanted to do so, but nothing seemed to work very well. The chimps were consistently able to get the bananas they wanted.

Banana theft wasn't the only problem at Gombe. Disease plagued the camp. Not long after first arriving at camp in 1960, Goodall fell ill with malaria, a common but dangerous tropical disease. Then in 1966, a polio epidemic swept through villages near the reserve. The epidemic posed a particular danger to Goodall, who was pregnant with her first child, and many of the chimpanzees at Gombe were also affected.

Polio is caused by a virus that attacks the nerve cells of the brain and spinal cord. While some victims only suffer mild symptoms, such as headaches, nausea, and sore throats, others can develop permanent paralysis.

Faben, a male chimp who contracted and survived polio, was left paralyzed in one arm. However, he was able to adjust to the disability and went on to function without special difficulty. Although physically challenged, Faben did not shy away from community conflicts. When his brother, Figan, made a move for the high-ranking position of the community, Faben provided invaluable support, battling alongside Figan when necessary.

Goodall and her staff watched helplessly as some of their favorite creatures fell victims to the disease. Some permanently lost the use of limbs, and four lost their lives. Pfizer Laboratories lent a hand by donating vaccine to help the people and chimps who hadn't yet contracted the disease. Leakey arranged for an emergency flight to transport the vaccine to where it was needed.

Vaccinating the chimps proved problematic, however. The plan involved lacing bananas with the vaccine, which was made from a weak but live form of the polio virus. The idea behind the vaccinations was that if a weak form of the virus was ingested by a chimp, the creature would develop antibodies to fight the disease. But it was difficult to control how many bananas an individual chimp would eat. Dominant chimps often ate more food than the others. The researchers feared these animals would eat too much of the vaccine-laced bananas and actually contract polio rather than be prevented from getting the disease. But they had to take the chance. The immunization seemed to work, and the epidemic eventually died out.

In 1967, Goodall and her husband regularly visited other parts of Africa. Early that year, the couple went camping in Ngorongoro Crater in Tanzania. One evening, they waited inside their tent as their cook, Anyango, prepared their evening meal. Suddenly, they heard loud noises that sounded like the clattering and banging of pots and pans. The sound of ripping tent canvas followed.

Peeking out of the tent, van Lawick saw a lion

The huge Ngorongoro Crater is 14 miles (22.4 km) across at its widest point and 2,000 feet (610 m) deep.

standing between their tent and their Land Rover. After closing up the tent again, he and Goodall heard the sounds of quick footsteps followed by the opening and slamming shut of a car door. Van Lawick opened the tent again, and when he saw no lion, ran to the Land Rover. Inside, he found an unharmed Anyango and Thomas, a worker who helped with odd jobs around the camp.

After the adventure with the lions, Goodall's African friends told her that she should name her baby Simba, the Swahili word for lion.

Slowly, van Lawick drove the Land Rover to his tent. Goodall, now eight months pregnant, safely got in the vehicle. After switching on the headlights, the frightened group saw the three young lions that had invaded their camp. With their vehicle, they began herding them away.

After the lions had been chased away, the group came back to camp only to discover one of the tents on fire. In her haste to scamper to safety, Goodall had left the flap of her tent open, and it had blown against the stove. The fire was quickly extinguished, but the group couldn't stay in the damaged tents. So they packed their essential gear and drove to a nearby cabin that they knew was empty. As they neared the cabin, the group saw a large lion lying on the veranda and a lioness in the back eating a freshly killed antelope. The lion eventually left, and the group was able to safely enter the cabin without bothering the lioness.

The next adventure in Goodall's life would come the following month. On March 4, 1967, Goodall gave birth to a healthy baby boy, Hugo Eric Louis van Lawick. The baby was soon nicknamed Grub. Jane felt it was important to make her son her top priority, so while he was a small child she cut back on her work with the chimps. Although mornings were spent with the researchers or writing,

> *Goodall took parenting cues from her observations of a chimp mother named Flo. She tried to follow Flo's patient example as she cared for her young son. Goodall wrote, "Mothers who were, like Flo, playful, affectionate, tolerant, and above all supportive, seemed to raise offspring who, as adults, had good relaxed relationships with community members. Mothers who were more harsh, less caring, less playful ... raised individuals who, as adults tended to be tense and ill at ease."*

Goodall's afternoons were devoted to her son.

During the course of the year, Goodall spent a great deal of time in the city of Nairobi. There Goodall met visitors who flew in to meet with her and visit Gombe. She also brought equipment to Nairobi to be repaired and conducted interviews for research assistants and other needed staff members. Since they were spending so much time in the city, Goodall and her husband decided to buy a home in Limuru, a suburb of Nairobi. In February, she wrote to her family about touring the beautiful home and meeting the man who was selling it. She particularly loved the view the home afforded from a large porch:

> *Built on by the last owner, behind [the kitchen and a bedroom], a built in veranda running the whole length of the house, windows all round, and a tiled floor. A really lovely room—you could use it for anything—sitting in, eating, having a party, for children or pets—or anything else you can think of! It made me smile to myself when the owner turned to Hugo and said, "It's a good room for the wife to sit with her sewing!"*

In February 1968, Goodall's beloved David Greybeard disappeared. By the time she returned to Gombe in June, it was assumed he had died during an epidemic that had claimed some of the chimps in his community. "When David disappeared during an epidemic of pneumonia in 1968, I mourned for him as I have no other chimpanzee before or since," Goodall later wrote.

In mid-August, Goodall recovered from her second bout of malaria in five years. Van Lawick had caught the disease before her, but Grub remained healthy.

That fall, Goodall and her family were back in Ngorongoro. As her husband went out on photo assignments, Goodall studied new favorite creatures—hyenas. Because hyenas are most active at night, she watched them by moonlight safe

A pair of hyena pups

> *Hyenas are known for their unusual howls, which sound very similar to human laughter. They are good hunters and sport strong jaws and teeth that allow them to crush and eat the bones of their prey. The spotted hyena ranks as the most common hyena and is found in Africa. Striped hyenas also are found in northern Africa, but they are smaller than spotted hyenas.*

inside a Volkswagen bus. As she sat in the front and observed the hyenas, Grub slept peacefully in the back of the bus. Goodall loved the quiet time spent with her son and watching these creatures of the night. Goodall wrote about the hyenas in a letter to her family on October 12, 1968:

> *Oh to see these gross old ladies, their stomachs only inches from the ground, gamboling after each other and frolicking with the pups in the moonlight! It is a sight that must be seen to be believed!*

But Goodall and her husband had to be especially careful now that they had a son. Many wild animals, including chimpanzees, had been known to take African babies as food. Before Grub learned to walk, they built a cage-like structure to protect the area where he slept at Gombe. At their Gombe beach house, they caged in the veranda so Grub could play unharmed.

The danger at Gombe didn't just come from the wild animals that lived there. The rough terrain commanded respect as well. Ruth Davies,

an American student studying the relationships of male chimpanzees at Gombe, became a victim of the dangerous terrain. When she didn't return to camp one summer day in 1969, the staff quickly grew worried. More than 300 people eventually joined the search for Davies. Her body was found in a ravine far from camp. She had fallen and died instantly from a fractured skull. Davies' death, however, wouldn't be the only cause of sadness in Gombe. ❧

Although beautiful, the African jungle is filled with deep ravines and rocky cliffs, making the terrain dangerous.

7 DISTURBING DISCOVERIES

⟨⟨✕⟩⟩

Goodall saw chimpanzees comfort one another when they were scared. She observed them kissing, hugging, and patting each other on their backs when they hadn't seen one another in a long time. She also watched older chimps adopt orphans. But not everything she and her researchers observed was positive. In the 1970s, she heard about and saw behaviors that saddened her. They included acts of cannibalism and war.

On September 15, 1971, a researcher noted the first signs of cannibalism among chimpanzees. The researcher saw a group of males attack a mother from another group. The males then took the chimp's baby and ate it.

Goodall, herself, witnessed attacks she found

even more disturbing. A female named Passion captured and killed two baby chimps, the offspring of another female within the same group. In another attack, Passion and her daughter, Pom, attacked Gilka, who suffered from polio. After wrestling the weakened chimp's daughter Otta from her grip, Passion killed the baby for her and Pom to feed on. The following year, Passion and Pom did the same to Gilka's next baby.

Goodall also witnessed signs of war among the chimps. In the early 1970s, the chimps she had been studying began breaking into two separate groups. The split happened gradually during the course of many months. However, they all continued visiting the banana-feeding area, which started to cause problems. The original group, called the Kasakela, lived in the north. Those who had separated, the Kahama, lived to the south. As early as 1971, noisy, angry displays were shown if one group found the other group in the feeding area. Even those who had been friends before the split eventually grew to hate one another.

Though they can't speak in words, chimpanzees communicate through a variety of calls and through body language. Chimpanzees each have a distinctive voice that is recognized by other chimps in their group. Chimpanzees also can learn American Sign Language. Some have learned as many as 300 words and use these signs to communicate with other chimps as well as with their trainers.

Males patrolled their new borders and sometimes invaded the territory of the other group.
If single chimps were found alone and unable to
protect themselves, the males attacked them. By
November 11, 1977, the Kasakela males killed the
last of the Kahama males. The remaining females
rejoined the original group, bringing to an end the
Kahamas. This marked the first time warfare had

ever been documented in nonhuman primates. Goodall said:

> *When I first started at Gombe, I thought the chimps were nicer than [humans] are. But time has revealed that they are not. They can be just as awful.*

Although most mother chimps are attentive, Goodall identified Fifi as an exceptionally caring mother.

But Goodall found that the chimpanzees also displayed strong bonds with one another. Especially strong were the bonds between brothers and those

between mothers and children.

For example, when Flo, the beloved mother chimp, died in 1972, her 8-year-old son, Flint, grew depressed. Goodall later wrote:

> *Never shall I forget watching as three days after Flo's death, Flint climbed slowly into a tall tree near the stream. He walked along one of the branches, then stopped and stood motionless, staring down at an empty nest. ... The nest was one which he and Flo had shared a short while before Flo died. What had he thought of as he stood there, staring? ... We shall never know.*

In the chimpanzee community, the mothers are responsible for raising the young. They will generally nurse their infants for three years, and when the babies are no longer dependent on the milk, the infants will normally show more independence. No special relationship exists with the fathers, but older males sometimes "adopt" younger brothers or sisters who have been orphaned.

Unlike most chimps his age, Flint never really detached from Flo to find his own way. After Flo died, Flint stayed near her body and refused to eat. Less than a month after his mother's death, an otherwise healthy Flint died, too. ✒

8 PROFESSOR GOODALL

Chapter

❧✦❧

The 1970s proved to be a time of great change for Goodall. In 1971, she was named a visiting professor at Stanford University in California. Her goal was to add primate studies to a new human biology major offered at the university.

During the next four years, Goodall traveled to Stanford twice a year to give lectures and work with students. In time, the Stanford Outdoor Primate Facility was built, giving students a chance to study captive chimps rescued from labs and others places. Students also had the opportunity to travel to Gombe and study chimps in their natural habitats.

Changes also occurred in Goodall's personal life in the early 1970s. She and van Lawick drifted apart, and, though they remained friends, they divorced in

Goodall cherished spending time with her son, Grub.

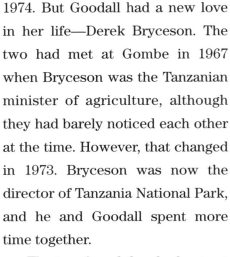

Human biology students study a wide variety of fields to learn about the biology and social and cultural behaviors of humans. Classes in Stanford University's human biology major range from a course on health care in America to cell biology to sports medicine. Most graduates continue their studies in advanced programs after earning their four-year degrees.

1974. But Goodall had a new love in her life—Derek Bryceson. The two had met at Gombe in 1967 when Bryceson was the Tanzanian minister of agriculture, although they had barely noticed each other at the time. However, that changed in 1973. Bryceson was now the director of Tanzania National Park, and he and Goodall spent more time together.

The two found they had a great deal in common. Along with a love of nature, Bryceson didn't let misfortunes stop him from living his life to the fullest. He'd been a fighter pilot in Britain's Royal Air Force during World War II and had been shot down in the Middle East when he was 19. Almost completely paralyzed from the waist down, Bryceson survived the crash but was told he'd never walk again. However, he proved his doctors wrong. Though walking would always be difficult, he re-taught himself the skill with the use of a cane.

Bryceson had moved to Kenya in 1946. He farmed for several years before becoming involved in politics. He eventually settled in a beach house at Dar es Salaam, which is where he lived when he and

The harbor at Dar es Salaam

Goodall fell in love. However, their love affair was nearly cut short by another plane crash, this time on a trip to Ruaha National Park. In a small, four-seater plane, Bryceson, Goodall, and Grub watched helplessly as the pilot crash-landed before he reached the runway. Goodall wrote to her mother about the crash in January 1974:

> *We crash landed at Ruaha and the plane was a write off. To this day we don't know how we ended up not only alive, but even unhurt—except that Derek got a bruised (probably cracked) rib. … Since so few people ever crash at all, and certainly so few survive the kind of ruined plane that we got out of—we feel confident that we are now safe. The people here have been telling me that God wanted us to finish*

our work to help them in Tanzania. It is like an omen, and I feel quite strange about it. For me, Africa has always been the ruling force of my life, I suppose. Now it is even more than that. Lots of things seem to have fallen into shape after nearly being dead—you know, you suddenly realize that it could happen (death, I mean) at any moment. So [you do] what is best to do with the life entrusted to you.

The brush with death led Goodall and Bryceson to cherish life even more than they had before. In February 1975, they got married.

Bryceson was by Goodall's side when a shocking incident occurred at Gombe. On May 19, 1975, a terrorist from Zaire named Laurent Kabila engineered the kidnapping of people from the Gombe camp. During the night, 40 armed men who were followers of Kabila attacked the African staff at Gombe and demanded to know where the white staff members were. Despite severe beatings, the African

Laurent Kabila (1939–2001)

staff members refused to answer. This didn't stop the terrorists, however. They searched until they found the students' huts.

The terrorists beat and bound three newly arrived Stanford students—two female and one male. They also kidnapped a female staff member. Others escaped capture by hiding in the woods. Goodall and Grub slept in a beach house less than a mile away, but they heard nothing. Once the kidnappers left, the students woke Goodall and told her what had happened.

Located in the center of Africa, Zaire became known as Congo in 1997 after rebels led by Laurent Kabila, the man who planned the Gombe kidnappings, seized control of the country. Kabila served as president of Congo until he was assassinated by a bodyguard. Today, the country is ruled by Kabila's son Joseph.

After the kidnapping, all those at the Gombe camp who were not from Tanzania were evacuated. Goodall and Bryceson were only allowed occasional visits to the research site. They lived in their home in Dar es Salaam and stayed in radio contact with the remaining staff in Gombe. Tanzanian field assistants continued following the lives of the chimpanzees and baboons to make sure Goodall's work wasn't interrupted.

After a week, one of the captured students, Barbara Smuts, who is today a well-known primatologist, was released, along with a list of the terrorists' demands. They wanted guns, freedom for other terrorists who had been imprisoned, and a ransom of around $500,000.

On May 27, 1975, Goodall sent a letter to the three remaining captives. She knew the terrorists would read the letter first, so she had to choose her words carefully. She wanted to give her friends hope and still show them she realized how serious their situation was. She also took care to make sure the captors wouldn't be offended by anything she wrote:

> *We are all thinking of you, we are praying for you, all over the world. Everyone, everywhere, all sending love and prayers and hoping and hoping that you are still well in mind and body. ... We all feel that the most important thing for your captors is to gain world sympathy. Surely they must know that this is their chance—that by treating you well and by returning you safely to your families, the world will be most impressed in their favour. On the other hand, if they harm you, the world will be shocked and the whole operation could bring them to a much worse position than they were in before they started it. ... Please try not to worry about your future. Everything is going to be all right. All the world feels certain that your captors are humane people. We are doing all that we can do. Please believe us and try to have faith.*

Six weeks after the kidnapping, one of the hostages' parents took out an emergency loan to pay the ransom, but the terrorists only released the women. They kept Steven Smith, the final captive student, to maintain pressure on the Tanzanian government to release the terrorist prisoners. It is unknown whether or not the government gave in to the demand, but a month later Smith was released.

Money had always been tight in Gombe, and some grant resources dried up after the kidnappings. Goodall worked hard to raise money by lecturing. Help came from good friends in 1976. An Italian nobleman and his wife, Prince Ranieri and Princess Genevieve di san Faustino, started a nonprofit organization called the Jane Goodall Institute for

The Jane Goodall Institute's Gombe location employs many Tanzanians.

Wildlife Research, Education and Conservation, giving Goodall more financial security for the future.

Goodall also wanted a secure future for her son, and the climate at Gombe was still considered dangerous. So that year, when Grub turned 9, she sent him to England to live with her mother. In Africa, Grub studied with tutors, but now he would go to a school where he would have classmates and teachers. Goodall would miss her young son, but she spent every holiday with him except for those he spent with his father. With Grub in safe hands, Goodall continued her work.

Gombe is a great source of peace for Goodall.

But in 1980, Bryceson died from cancer. Goodall went back to England for a while before returning to Tanzania and her chimpanzees. During her first two days back, it was difficult for her to be alone in the house she had shared with her husband. But on the third morning her spirits lifted.

After my lonely cup of coffee ... I set off to find the chimps. And as I climbed the steep slope to the feeding station, suddenly I found I was smiling. I was on the part of the trail that Derek, with his paralyzed legs, had found so difficult and tiring. But now it was I, the earth-bound one, who was struggling in the heat—he was light and free. He was teasing me so that I laughed out loud.

Like always, Gombe was a place where Goodall could feel at home. 🐾

9 Chapter MAKING LIFE BETTER FOR CHIMPS EVERYWHERE

⤥⟊⟊⟊⟋⟋⟋

In 1986, animal rights activists secretly filmed conditions at a research lab called Sema, Inc., where about 500 primates were housed. The tapes were sent to People for the Ethical Treatment of Animals (PETA). From the tapes, PETA produced a short documentary called *Breaking Barriers* and sent copies to people they believed would be interested, including Goodall.

Throughout her career, Goodall had avoided visiting such labs. She believed there was nothing she could do to help these animals. But after seeing *Breaking Barriers*, Goodall knew she had to try. She recalled:

> *The first laboratory I ever visited was*

Founded in 1980, PETA, with 850,000 members, now ranks as the largest animal-rights organization in the world. Members of PETA work to protect the rights of all animals, sometimes using controversial methods to gain attention. They do not believe animals should be used in experiments, for entertainment, or for food or clothing. Public education, cruelty investigations, research, animal rescue, legislation, special events, celebrity involvement, and protest campaigns are some of the ways that PETA members work to fulfill their mission.

just outside America's capital, in Rockville, Maryland. I had seen a videotape taken during an illicit entry, but even so I was not prepared for the nightmare world into which I was ushered by smiling, white-coated men.

She had asked for permission to tour Sema, which welcomed her in March 1987. Conditions at the company sickened her. She saw animals in cages so small the creatures could barely move. Chimps that had been injected with diseases such as HIV and hepatitis were isolated from the other animals. Some of the chimps stayed alone in cages, with no contact with other chimps for as long as the study lasted—sometimes as long as three years.

Goodall visited other medical research labs as well. Conditions varied greatly. While some were as bad as Sema, others impressed her with the great care they gave their animals and their openness to making things even better. Goodall went to work to make all labs that used animals as humane as possible. She brought attention to the problems

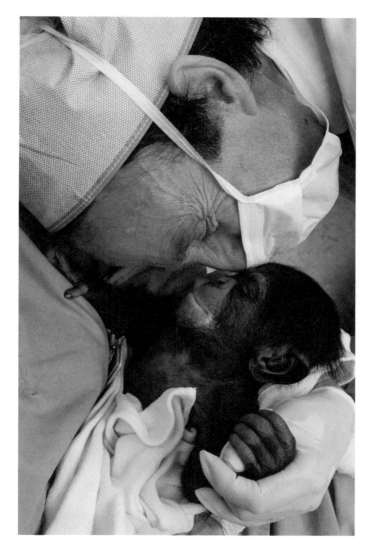

and talked about the issue at her lectures. She wrote an opinion piece for *The New York Times Magazine.* And while she would rather see experiments on animals stopped entirely, she focused on improving treatment of the lab animals rather than getting into an argument about the value of using animals in medical research.

Goodall also has brought attention to other threats to chimpanzees. Africa's chimpanzee population is in jeopardy because their habitats are being eliminated. In some cases, rain forests are cut down to make expensive furniture. In other cases, land is cleared to make way for more farmland. In either case, without the trees, the land eventually

A bulldozer clears trees and other vegetation in an African rain forest.

loses its nutrients, nothing grows there anymore, and the chimps lose their home. Clearing away more trees for new farmland and leaving this "dead" land barren only adds to the problem. As the land erodes away into rivers and lakes, fish populations are killed. In the end, people suffer and starve as the animals die and the land becomes useless.

> *The exploding growth of the human population is another reason for the decline of chimp habitats. The population of Africa is doubling at a rate of every 24 years, leading to great demands on natural resources.*

Another problem for the chimpanzee population is that chimps are hunted for food, and in some cases, mothers are killed so their babies can be sold to zoos or circuses or as pets or lab animals. Goodall wrote:

> *I can never forget the first time I saw one of these pathetic infants for sale in the tourist market of a Central African town. He had a piece of cord tied tightly around his waist, and this was attached to the top of a tiny wire cage. He was curled up on his side, and when I went close, I saw that he was sweating in the heat. His eyes were dull and staring into space. It would not be long before he was dead.*

Goodall knew if she bought the chimp, she'd only give the seller more reason to go out and capture another. Instead, she went to see the American ambassador, and together they visited the minister for the environment. Though hunting and selling chimps without a license is illegal, no one makes a fuss when it's done. Because of this, the law is rarely enforced. Goodall made sure that it was enforced this time. The environmental minister and a police officer visited the market with Goodall and confiscated the injured, frightened infant.

Goodall dubbed the chimp Little Jay. Her friend Graziella Cotman agreed to nurse him back to health. In time, more infant chimps were confiscated under the law, and Cotman agreed to help them. Through the generosity of the petroleum company Conoco, the Tchimpounga Sanctuary was built for these chimps in Central Africa. Because they were taken from their mothers so young, these chimps never learned the skills they needed for survival in the wild. For them, the sanctuary, a fenced-in forest area, is the best that can be done. Here they are safe from other chimps that might not accept

The Jane Goodall Institute opened a second chimpanzee sanctuary in 1998. The Ngamba Island Sanctuary originally housed 19 chimpanzees that were moved from the Uganda Wildlife Education Center and Queen Elizabeth National Park. While these organizations offered an ample habitat, the Ngamba Island Sanctuary provided 97 acres (38.8 hectares) of space for the chimps to live. By providing a safe place for the chimps, the Jane Goodall Institute hopes to preserve the chimp population in Uganda. At the end of 2005, 42 chimps resided on Ngamba Island.

TIONAL PRESS CLUB

them, and they always have a safe supply of food and trees to climb. Since then, more sanctuaries have been set up near other African communities.

Goodall also works to improve the lives of captive chimpanzees. Founded in 1984, the ChimpanZoo Project documents the lives of captive chimps and promotes happy, healthy environments for them. The project also strives to educate the public on the plight of chimpanzees and increase understanding of their behavior. 🐾

Goodall never ceases working for the animals she loves. In 1985, she served as honorary chairperson of the World Wildlife Fund's campaign to raise $1 million for primates.

10 CONTINUING TO SPREAD THE WORD

❧❦☙

Jane Goodall has spent more than 45 years of her life studying chimpanzees and furthering the cause of all animals and their environments throughout the world. Along with being the subject of many articles and books, she's written many herself, including the best sellers *In the Shadow of Man* and *Reason for Hope: A Spiritual Journey.*

For her work, Goodall has earned many honors. Among them are the National Geographic Society's Hubbard Medal, the Albert Schweitzer Award from the Animal Welfare Institute in Washington, D.C., and Japan's Kyoto Prize in Basic Science.

Though much less of her time is spent with the animals she loves in Gombe, Goodall continues her work in other ways.

When Goodall travels she often carries a stuffed chimp named Mr. H. with her. He is her personal mascot.

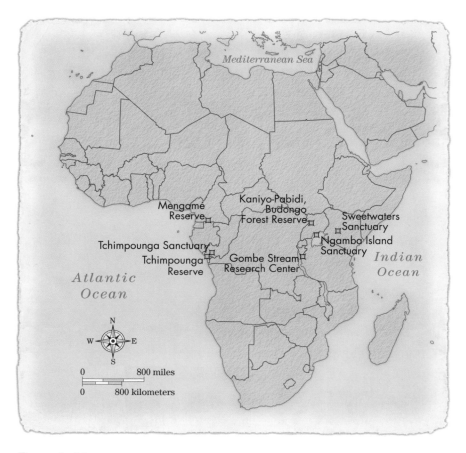

Mediterranean Sea

Mengame
Reserve

Kaniyo-Pabidi,
Budongo
Forest Reserve

Sweetwaters
Sanctuary

Tchimpounga Sanctuary

Ngamba Island
Sanctuary

Tchimpounga
Reserve

Gombe Stream
Research Center

*Indian
Ocean*

*Atlantic
Ocean*

N
W E
S

0   800 miles

0   800 kilometers

The work of the Jane Goodall Institute's African programs stretches across the continent.

Through the Lake Tanganyika Catchment Reforestation and Education (TACARE) program, Goodall encourages reforestation of Tanzania. The program also provides education and promotes conservation. Through TACARE, area villagers are offered help in setting up nurseries where they can grow trees to replace those that have been chopped down. If rain forests can be saved, Goodall believes tourism can bring more money into Africa and help end the problems of poverty and starvation.

Among Goodall's proudest accomplishments is the creation of Roots & Shoots, a program devoted to inspiring young people to become active in their communities around the globe. She wrote:

> *My greatest hope lies in the fact that young people, all around the world, are not only aware of the problems, but actually want to try to help solve them. And because the future of the planet lies in the hands of today's and tomorrow's youth, I decided I wanted to do my share of trying to help you to help the world. My way of helping was to start Roots & Shoots.*

The program started in 1991 with a group of children in Dar es Salaam. In 1993, it spread to the United States and Europe. Today, more than 50 countries boast Roots & Shoots chapters. They also are found in nearly every state in the United States. Members range in age from preschool through college students.

Each Roots & Shoots group is unique. Members decide what the goals of their individual group should be, based on their community's needs. Some plant trees or collect trash, while others collect clothes for the homeless or visit children in hospitals. What the groups have in common is that they are working toward making the world a better place.

Goodall said:

> *I think Roots & Shoots is probably the reason I came into the world. Yet I couldn't have done it without all those years with the chimpanzees and an understanding that led to a blurring of the line between "man" and "beast." Children give me particular hope because they have more open minds. They aren't as set in their ways. Only if children grow up with respect for all living things will the planet have a chance for survival.*

Goodall also continues to lecture around the world. People flock to hear her stories about life with the chimpanzees, and she also uses these opportunities to educate her audiences. Her hope is that people will come away from her lectures with an increased appreciation for nature and a desire to help preserve it.

Today, some of Goodall's favorite time is still spent among her chimps in Gombe. She wrote:

> *Although the chimps who used to live in the forests all along the lake shore have gone, along with the trees that were their home, the chimpanzees of Gombe are safe. When I go to visit them I can escape into the forest world I know so well and love so much. It's a world of entwined branches, soft colors in shades of brown and green*

and yellow. I always get new strength from the forest and also a sense of peace that I can take with me, back into the hurly-burly of the lecture-tour world.

Chimps, like this male named Wilkie, have provided Goodall with her important life's work.

Though the world has changed a great deal since Jane Goodall first set foot on the reserve, this little piece of paradise remains, thanks to her hard work. ᴥ

GOODALL'S LIFE

1934

Born April 3 in London, England

1941

Reads *The Story of Doctor Dolittle* and decides she must go to Africa someday

1957

In April, travels to Kenya to visit a friend; on May 24, meets Louis Leakey and starts working as his secretary

1933

Nazi leader Adolf Hitler is named chancellor of Germany

1939

German troops invade Poland; Britain and France declare war on Germany; World War II (1939–1945) begins

1953

The first Europeans climb Mount Everest

WORLD EVENTS

1960

On July 16, arrives at Gombe with her mother, Vanne, and African cook Dominic Charles Bandola

1961

Is visited by David Greybeard for the first time

1963

In December, first article is published in *National Geographic*

1960

1959

Fidel Castro becomes leader of Cuba

1961

The Berlin Wall is built, dividing East and West Germany

1963

Kenya becomes an independent republic with Jomo Kenyatta as its first president

GOODALL'S LIFE

1964

Marries Hugo van Lawick on March 28

1966

Earns Ph.D. from Cambridge University in April

1967

Son, Hugo, is born on March 4

1965

1966

The National Organization for Women (NOW) is established to work for equality between women and men

1967

The first heart transplant is attempted

WORLD EVENTS

1968

Scholarly article on the Gombe chimps is published in *Animal Behavior Monographs;* it goes on to become an academic classic

1974

Divorces Hugo van Lawick

1975

In February, marries Derek Bryceson; on May 19, a terrorist group kidnaps four people from Goodall's Gombe camp; they are later released

1975

1968

Civil rights leader Martin Luther King Jr. and U.S. presidential candidate Robert F. Kennedy are assassinated two months apart

1974

Scientists find that chlorofluorocarbons—chemicals in coolants and propellants—are damaging Earth's ozone layer

GOODALL'S LIFE

1976

Jane Goodall
Institute for
Wildlife Research,
Education and
Conservation is
established

1980

Derek Bryceson
dies

1984

ChimpanZoo
Project begins

1980

1979

The Soviet Union
invades Afghanistan

1983

The AIDS (acquired
immune deficiency
syndrome) virus is
identified

1982

Maya Lin designs the
Vietnam War Memorial,
commemorating
Americans who died

WORLD EVENTS

1990

Earns the Kyoto Prize in Basic Science

1991

Establishes Roots & Shoots in Dar es Salaam

2005

In September, inaugurates Roots & Shoots Day of Peace in Jackson Hole, Wyoming

1990

1990

Political prisoner Nelson Mandela, a leader of the anti-apartheid movement in South Africa, is released; Mandela becomes president of South Africa in 1994

1991

The Soviet Union collapses and is replaced by the Commonwealth of Independent States

2005

Major earthquake kills thousands in Pakistan

FULL NAME: Valerie Jane Morris-Goodall

DATE OF BIRTH: April 3, 1934

BIRTHPLACE: London, England

FATHER: Mortimer Morris-Goodall

MOTHER: Margaret "Vanne" Myfanwe Morris-Goodall

EDUCATION: Ph.D. from Cambridge University

FIRST SPOUSE: Hugo van Lawick (1937–2002)

DATE OF MARRIAGE: March 28, 1964

CHILDREN: Hugo Eric Louis van Lawick (1967–)

SECOND SPOUSE: Derek Bryceson (?–1980)

DATE OF MARRIAGE: February 1975

FURTHER READING

Goodall, Jane. *The Chimpanzees I Love: Saving Their World and Ours.* New York: Scholastic Press, 2001.

Goodall, Jane. *My Life with the Chimpanzees.* New York: Byron Preiss Visual Publications, Inc., 2002.

Lindsey, Jennifer. *Jane Goodall: 40 Years at Gombe: A Tribute to Four Decades of Wildlife Research, Education, and Conservation.* New York: Stewart, Tabori & Chang, 2000.

Pettit, Jayne. *Jane Goodall: Pioneer Researcher.* New York: Franklin Watts, 1999.

Pratt, Paula. *Jane Goodall.* San Diego: Lucent Books, 1997.

LOOK FOR MORE SIGNATURE LIVES
BOOKS ABOUT THIS ERA:

Benazir Bhutto: *Pakistani Prime Minister and Activist*
ISBN 0-7565-1578-5

Fidel Castro: *Leader of Communist Cuba*
ISBN 0-7565-1580-7

Winston Churchill: *British Soldier, Writer, Statesman*
ISBN 0-7565-1582-3

Adolf Hitler: *Dictator of Nazi Germany*
ISBN 0-7565-1589-0

Queen Noor: *American-born Queen of Jordan*
ISBN 0-7565-1595-5

Eva Perón: *First Lady of Argentina*
ISBN 0-7565-1585-8

Joseph Stalin: *Dictator of the Soviet Union*
ISBN 0-7565-1597-1

On the Web

For more information on *Jane Goodall*, use FactHound.

1. Go to *www.facthound.com*
2. Type in a search word related to this book or this book ID: 0756515904
3. Click on the *Fetch It* button.

FactHound will fetch the best Web sites for you.

Historic Sites

Natural History Museum of
Los Angeles County
900 Exposition Blvd.
Los Angeles, CA 90007
213/763-3466
An exhibit of African mammals in their natural environments

North Carolina Zoo
4401 Zoo Parkway
Asheboro, NC 27205
800/488-0444
A member of the Jane Goodall Institute's ChimpanZoo program; includes a chimpanzee exhibit that combines large trees, thick vegetation, and termite mounds to make an environment similar to a tropical forest

cud
swallowed food returned to the mouth from the cow's stomach for more chewing

encroachment
a gradual take over of land

gamboling
leaping around while playing

ingested
eaten

perseverance
the act of continually trying or committing to a certain action or belief

preconceived
formed before experience or evidence

primates
members of the group of intelligent mammals that includes humans, monkeys, apes, and lemurs

renowned
well known and respected

Chapter 2

Page 17, line 8: Jennifer Lindsey. *Jane Goodall: 40 Years at Gombe.* New York: Stewart, Tabori & Chang, 2000, p. 18.

Page 20, line 2: Jane Goodall. *My Life with the Chimpanzees.* New York: Byron Preiss Visual Publications, Inc., 2002, pp. 14–15.

Chapter 3

Page 25, line 12: Ibid., p. 28.

Page 27, line 1: Ibid., p. 29

Page 28, line 13: Ibid., p. 33.

Page 30, line 4: Jane Goodall. *Africa in My Blood: An Autobiography in Letters: The Early Years.* Boston: Houghton Mifflin Company, 2000, p. 1.

Page 32, line 5: Ibid., p. 108.

Page 37, line 4: Ibid., p. 145.

Chapter 4

Page 39, line 8: *My Life with the Chimpanzees*, p. 58.

Chapter 5

Page 46, line 1: *Africa in My Blood: An Autobiography in Letters: The Early Years*, pp. 163-164.

Page 52, line 14: Ibid., p. 190.

Chapter 6

Page 61, sidebar: Jane Goodall. *Reason for Hope: A Spiritual Journey.* New York: Warner Books, Inc., 1999, p. 89.

Page 62, line 15: Jane Goodall. *Beyond Innocence: An Autobiography in Letters: The Later Years.* Boston: Houghton Mifflin Company, 2001, p. 42.

Page 63, line 2: *Jane Goodall: 40 Years at Gombe*, p. 30.

Page 64, line 10: *Beyond Innocence: An Autobiography in Letters: The Later Years*, p. 112.

Chapter 7

Page 70, line 3: *Jane Goodall: 40 Years at Gombe*, p. 64.

Page 71, line 6: Jane Goodall. *Through a Window: My Thirty Years with the Chimpanzees of Gombe.* Boston: Houghton Mifflin Company, 1990, p. 196.

Chapter 8

Page 75, line 8: *Beyond Innocence: An Autobiography in Letters: The Later Years*, pp. 239-240.

Page 78, line 10: Ibid., pp. 186-187.

Page 81, line 7: *Reason for Hope: A Spiritual Journey*, p. 162.

Chapter 9

Page 83, line 14: Ibid., p. 311.

Page 87, line 16: *My Life with the Chimpanzees*, pp. 126-127.

Chapter 10

Page 93, line 6: Ibid., p. 141.

Page 94, line 2: *Jane Goodall: 40 Years at Gombe*, pp. 105-106.

Page 94, line 22: *My Life with the Chimpanzees*, p. 149.

Chu, Jeff. "The Queen of Gombe." *Time Europe.* 2 Oct. 2004. 6 Oct. 2005. www.time.com/time/europe/hero2004/goodall.html.

Facklam, Margery. *Wild Animals, Gentle Women.* New York: Harcourt Brace Javanovich, 1978.

Goodall, Jane. *Africa in My Blood: An Autobiography in Letters: The Early Years.* Boston: Houghton Mifflin Company, 2000.

Goodall, Jane. *Beyond Innocence: An Autobiography in Letters: The Later Years.* Boston: Houghton Mifflin Company, 2001.

Goodall, Jane. *Through a Window: My Thirty Years with the Chimpanzees of Gombe.* London: Phoenix Giant, 1998.

Goodall, Jane, with Phillip Berman. *Reason for Hope: A Spiritual Journey.* New York: Warner Books, 1999.

Jane Goodall: 40 Years at Gombe. Animal Planet. 6 Oct. 2005. http://animal.discovery.com/fansites/janegoodall/janegoodall.html.

The Jane Goodall Institute. 6 Oct. 2005. www.janegoodall.org.

"Jane Goodall's Wild Chimpanzees." PBS. 6 Oct. 2005. www.pbs.org/wnet/nature/goodall/.

Montgomery, Sy. *Walking with the Great Apes: Jane Goodall, Dian Fossey, Biruté Galdikas.* Boston: Houghton Mifflin Company, 1991.

National Geographic Online. 6 Oct. 2005. www.nationalgeographic.com.

Brenda Haugen started in the newspaper business and had a career as an award-winning journalist before finding her niche as an author. Since then, she has written and edited many books, most of them for children. A graduate of the University of North Dakota in Grand Forks, Brenda lives in North Dakota with her family.